SPIN now!

SPIN NOW!

THE DJ STARTER HANDBOOK

DJ Shortee

HAL•LEONARD®
Hal Leonard Books
An Imprint of Hal Leonard Corporation

Published in 2012 by Hal Leonard Books
An Imprint of Hal Leonard Corporation
7777 West Bluemound Road
Milwaukee, WI 53213

Trade Book Division Editorial Offices
33 Plymouth St., Montclair, NJ 07042

For photographs in the text, the author wishes to thank Rane, Shure, Pioneer, Technics, Alesis, Sennheiser, Stanton, Vestax, Serato, Native Instruments, Mixed In Key, FL Studio, Ortofon, Sony, Pearl Music, Zildjian, KRK, Beatport, TrackItDown, Soundcloud, and Facebook.

The image of the Camelot Wheel on page 50 is reprinted with permission of Mixed In Key. All rights reserved.

Printed in the United States of America
Book design by Kristina Rolander

Library of Congress Cataloging-in-Publication Data

DJ Shortee.
 Spin now! : the DJ starter handbook / DJ Shortee.
   pages cm
1. Disc jockeys--Vocational guidance. 2. Sound recording--Remixing. I. Title.
 ML3795.D57 2012
 781.4--dc23
                          2012002082

ISBN 978-1-4584-1652-0

www.halleonardbooks.com

To my partner in music and life, DJ Faust,
who taught me the basics of DJing.
Thank you for supporting me in every possible way
and pushing me to follow my dreams.

CONTENTS

SPIN
NOW!

1 WHAT IS A DJ?

A DJ IS ...

A DJ is someone who selects and plays musical recordings for an audience. The word *DJ* is short for *deejay* or *disc jockey,* originally referring to a person who played vinyl records. Nowadays DJs use a variety of different formats, including vinyl, CDs, and MP3s. (Yes, they still make vinyl!)

WHAT KIND OF DJ DO YOU WANT TO BE?

There are different types of DJs, and the role of each DJ really depends on the job.

CLUB DJ

A club DJ is someone who plays music in nightclubs, raves, and bars. Some stick to one genre of music and only play events that promote that genre, while others spin multiple genres. If you play commercial genres, you'll also be expected to work the mic to hype up the crowd, take requests, and announce birthdays and bachelorette parties. Resident DJs play the same venue on a regular basis and may open or close for headlining guest DJs or play the entire event on their own. Traveling DJs are guest DJs who travel to perform at different venues in various cities and countries around the world. Many are also producers or remixers with a substantial fan base who are known to provide a certain unique sound. Superstar DJs are the elite traveling DJs who have achieved a household name within their music scene and are making a ton of money jet-setting around the world, playing massive events, and living out their dreams. All DJs should shoot for the stars. But don't worry—even if you don't hit superstar status, you can still make a decent living as a club DJ and it's a lot of fun!

MOBILE DJ

A mobile DJ brings an entire sound system and lighting rig to the event, sets it up, and runs the whole show solo. Events include weddings, Bar Mitzvahs, proms, birthdays, holiday parties, and so on. The music is generally commercial and well known, and the occasion may be very special to the client. Personality, versatility, and ingenuity are must-haves because you'll have to adapt to any situation and literally get the party started with a diverse group of people who may be shy to let loose. You may have to provide a Karaoke setup, start party games to get people involved, and announce special moments, requests, or dedications. It's a ton of work, expensive, and you'll probably be playing the same songs over and over. But the business payoff can be huge, and you'll become a master at reading and controlling a crowd.

RADIO DJ

Radio personalities introduce and play music that is broadcast on AM, FM, shortwave, digital, or Internet radio stations. DJs usually play the tracks one by one from beginning to end according to the station's playlist; however, some also mix the songs into one another continuously, just like in a nightclub. Radio is intimate because you're relating to the listeners one on one, so your personality and speech presence is important and you should talk to them like you would to a close friend sitting beside you. Additional responsibilities may include announcing commercials, punching in audio sweeps, interviewing talent, taking requests, and connecting with listeners via phone or Internet.

SUPPORTING DJ

These DJs back up an artist onstage and play the artist's instrumental music for them. This started in hip-hop when rappers performed with DJs who provided their music. Nowadays DJs support all kinds of musicians and vocalists in a variety of genres. When performing with a solo artist or a group, you may play a set list of their music, attend rehearsals, create remixes of the music to play at shows, scratch as a musician in the group, open and/or close out the show playing a DJ set, and go on tour with that artist or group. Some artists feature you as part of their show while others keep you in the background. Either way, the artist is the main focus and your job is to support them. If the artist is established, some cool perks may include performing in massive stadiums, appearing in their music videos, and performing with them on TV.

TURNTABLIST

A turntablist is a musician who plays the turntable (or CDJ) and mixer as an musical instrument, creating rhythms and melodies by hand, using advanced techniques such as scratching and beat juggling. Like playing any instrument, turntablism takes tons of practice and dedication and is very rewarding because you are actually creating music. That said, a turntablist alone is not a DJ. Some turntablists are strictly musicians who don't play DJ sets. However, most turntablists are also DJs and use their turntablist skills to accent their DJ performances. If you really want to take your DJ skills to the next level, learn some turntablist techniques! As Egyptian Lover says, "What is a DJ if he can't scratch?!"

2 TOOLS OF THE TRADE

So many buttons and knobs, oh my! Don't worry, the equipment may seem intimidating, but once you learn the basics it's easy. If you've ever played music on a radio, CD player, or iPod, you're already a step ahead of the game!

ESSENTIALS

You'll need music, something to play it on, a mixer to blend it together, and a pair of headphones so you can hear what you are doing. If you want other people to hear your music, you'll also need to get some speakers. That's pretty much it.

Need more info? What the heck is a mixer? Don't worry, I got you covered!

AUDIO

You have to have tunes to spin, right?! Your job as a DJ begins with studying your favorite genres and collecting quality music. Your unique sound is created by the music you choose to play. Be sure to regularly seek out music you love on records, CDs, and/or digital audio files such as MP3, WAV, or AIFF.

Sound

PLAYERS

Players used to manipulate and play music include turntables, CD players, MP3 players, and DJ software controllers. You'll need two of them or one that offers dual decks so that you can mix two songs together. You may also use a computer running a DJ software program offering virtual players. This type of software is definitely a money saver and the only space it takes up is on your hard drive. However, physically manipulating the music by hand adds so much more to your performance than just staring at a laptop and clicking a mouse. So if you've got the budget for it, get the hardware!

Technics 1210 Turntable

Stanton T.62B turntable

Pioneer CDJ-2000 CD Player

Pioneer CDJ-850 CD Player

Pioneer MEP-7000 Dual CD Player

VestaxVCl300 Controller

Pioneer DDJ-T1 Controller

Serato Scratch Live Software

Traktor Scratch Pro Software

MIXER

A DJ mixer acts as a go-between, allowing you to blend the audio from one player to another. It's also a preamplifier, boosting the audio signal and enabling you to control the music's volume. Pretty snazzy, eh?

Rane TTM57SL Mixer

Pioneer DJM-909 Mixer

Rane Sixtyeight Mixer

Pioneer DJM-900nexus Mixer

Rane TTM56 Mixer

Pioneer DJM-250 Mixer

AMPLIFIERS

Amps are used to increase the sound and send the audio signal to the speakers. There are now many consumer-grade speakers available that are self-powered with amps built in, so you may not need an amp; however, most nightclubs with large speaker systems use amplifiers.

Alesis Amp

SPEAKERS

Yup, that's right, folks: speakers make the music audible on the dance floor! They are a must-have if you want others to hear you DJing. (But you already knew that.)

KRK V8 Speaker

Pioneer
S-DJ08 Speaker

HEADPHONES

Those iPod headphones won't cut it in a loud nightclub, so you'll want to get a pair of DJ headphones that cup your ears and block outside sound. The better your headphones, the better you'll be able to hear what you're doing, and that's important!

Sennheiser HD-25-1
Headphones

Pioneer HDJ-2000
Headphones

MICROPHONE

If you want to talk to your audience, you'll need a mic. It amplifies your voice and sounds way better than just yelling over the music, hoping that people will understand what the heck you're trying to say.

Shure Beta 58A
Microphone

DIFFERENT TYPES OF GEAR

Check out these options and their specs to decide what's right for you.

TURNTABLES

Want to play vinyl records? You'll need a pair of turntables. The industry standards are Technics 1200 or 1210 because they're extremely durable, dependable, and last a long time. However, a lot of other brands make quality decks as well, so when you're checking them out, make sure they have the following features:

> **Quality Manufacturing.** Your decks need to be heavy so they don't move and shake the needle around while you are using them. A solid, well-built turntable also helps if you're playing in a loud setting because they

absorb any bass vibrations that might cause feedback. More importantly, since you're just starting out, quality turntables will make learning so much easier and more enjoyable. Crappy turntables are insanely frustrating to use no matter what your skill level, so don't even bother wasting your money on "cheaper" versions. Ultimately you'll end up spending more when you have to replace them because they suck.

» **Direct Drive.** The only turntables good for DJing are direct drive, meaning the platter is directly powered by the motor. Belt-driven turntables aren't an option because the motor powers a rubber belt, which makes the platter turn, and that just sucks for mixing records.

» **Powerful Torque.** Torque refers to how powerfully the motor spins the platter on the turntable. Your decks need a strong motor so that when you touch the record or stop it with your hand, the platter doesn't slow down or stop spinning underneath.

» **Pitch Control.** Your turntables need a dependable pitch control so the speed can be adjusted quickly and efficiently, and the tempo won't waver randomly once it's set.

A turntable and its basic features:

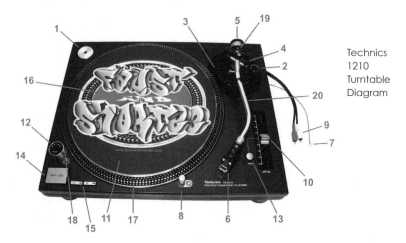

Technics 1210 Turntable Diagram

1 45 RPM ADAPTER: Fits around the spindle so that you can play those little 7-inch 45 records with the big holes.

2 ANTI-SKATING CONTROL KNOB: Keeps the needle in the groove so that it doesn't slide across the record.

3 ARM-HEIGHT ADJUSTMENT RING: Raises and lowers the tone arm.

4 ARM LOCK KNOB: Locks the height of the tone arm in place.

5 BALANCE WEIGHT (COUNTER BALANCE): Balances the weight of the tone arm and cartridge so that the needle stays on the record but doesn't dig into the grooves.

6 CARTRIDGE AND STYLUS (NEEDLE): Rides in the groves of the record and rubs along tiny bumps causing vibrations. The cartridge converts the vibrations into electrical signals, which become music.

7 GROUND WIRE: Grounds the electrical signal. Screw this into the back of your mixer to avoid horrible buzzing sounds.

8 LIGHT: Highlights where your needle is on the record.

9 PHONO WIRES: Right (red) and left (white) audio channels that you plug into the corresponding channels on your mixer.

10 PITCH CONTROL: Speeds up or slows down the rotation of the platter enabling you to match songs with different tempos. Faster is "+", Slower is "-". The range varies on different turntables (±8, ±16, and more). Longer pitch controls allow you to mix a wider range of tempos. A green light glows in the center when the turntable is playing at the zero point, which is the song's original tempo.

11 PLATTER: This platform spins the record around the spindle.

12 POWER SWITCH: Turns the turntable on and off.

13 QUARTZ LOCK: Locks the tempo at zero regardless of where the pitch slider is on the scale.

14 START/STOP BUTTON: Starts and stops turning the platter.

15 SPEED SELECT BUTTONS: Sets platter speed to 33 or 45 rotations per minute. The record's label should indicate play speed. (Those little ones with big holes play at 45.)

16 SPINDLE: Holds the record in place on the platter.

17 STROBE DOTS: Show how accurately your turntable is spinning. When you are exactly at 33 or 45 rpm they'll appear to stand still in the Strobe Light. If they don't it means the pitch control is out of tune or the motor may have problems.

18 STROBE LIGHT: Illuminates the strobe dots.

19 STYLUS PRESSURE RING: This numbered dial on the counter weight allows you calibrate the tone arm to "0" and shows how much weight you're adding to it.

20 TONEARM: Holds the needle on the record. It can be straight or S shaped. Screw the locking nut around the headshell connector to lock the needle in place,

Turntables also need ...

Needles (Cartridges)

The needle, or stylus, is a tiny diamond that rides along the record's grooves and vibrates against little bumps inside them. It connects to the cartridge, which converts the vibrations into electrical signals. These signals create the actual music.

TIP: DJ cartridges come complete with a stylus. However, if the needle breaks or wears down, you only have to replace the stylus itself and it's much cheaper than the total package.

As a beginner you'll probably knock them around while you're learning, so don't waste your money on high-end needles since they'll be replaced soon anyway. Most of the lower-end needles still have decent sound quality. The boxier designs made by Shure and Stanton are better at taking a beating.

Needle Options and Features

Styli and cartridges come in a few different flavors:

» **Spherical Stylus.** Perfect for vinyl manipulation such as back spinning and scratching because it's rounded, a spherical stylus doesn't tear up your vinyl as much and stays in the grooves better. It's also a good needle for a heavy-handed beginner because it tracks so well.

Spherical

» **Elliptical Stylus**. This shape produces a slightly better sound quality because it sits deeper in the grooves. However, it doesn't track as well, so it's best for those who aren't manipulating the record much.

Elliptical

» **All-in-One Cartridge.** Doesn't offer as many options for control. However, there's no assembly required—just plug and play!

» **Mounted Cartridge**. It's attached to a headshell; you can adjust the weight and position of the needle, giving you more control over its tracking abilities.

All-in-One:
Ortofon
S-120

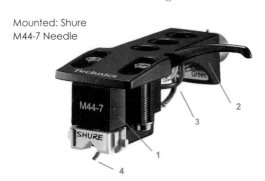

Mounted: Shure
M44-7 Needle

1 CARTRIDGE: Converts vibrations into electrical signals, which become music.

2 HEADSHELL: Holds everything in place and connects to the tone arm.

3 LEAD WIRES:
  • Red: Right Channel (R)
  • Green: Right Ground (RG)
  • White: Left Channel (L)
  • Blue: Left Ground (LG)

4 STYLUS AND STYLUS TIP: The little diamond that creates the vibrations by rubbing against the bumpy record grooves.

How to Assemble a Mounted Needle

1. Remove stylus from the cartridge if attached.

2. Use needle-nose pliers to connect the four colored lead wires from the tonearm headshell to the corresponding pins on the cartridge. (Red "right" wire connects to the "R" pin. Green "right ground" connects to "RG" pin ...)

3. Position cartridge flush to the front edge of the headshell and attach with screws (adding the weight in between, if desired).

Needle Assembly

4. Insert stylus into the cartridge.

How to Balance the Needle on the Tonearm

These directions are based on a Shure M44-7. Other needles may have different height and weight settings, so check the manual and apply those settings.

1. Attach needle to tonearm.

2. Set tonearm height to "4" by turning the arm-height adjustment ring clockwise until the little arrow points to the number.

Attaching the Cartridge on the Tonearm.

Tone Arm Height

Numbered Dial Toward Front

3. Position the counterweight so that the stylus pressure ring (i.e., the numbered dial on the weight) is toward the front.

4. Calibrate tonearm by adjusting counter-weight on the back until the tonearm floats parallel to the turntable, above the record, and the needle appears in perfect balance with the weight in the back.

Floating Tonearm

5. Hold weight in place and turn the stylus pressure ring until the "0" is centered at the top. The tonearm is now calibrated just like a scale so you know where the zero balance point is.

6. Set tracking force to 3.5 grams by rotating the entire weight until the "3.5" is centered at the top.

7. Set anti-skate control to zero by turning the anti-skate knob so that the "0" is touching the line.

Stylus Ring to "0"

Weight to "3.5"

Anti-Skate to Zero

3 Leveled and Unleveled Tonearms

TIP: Some turntables come with basic needles, so you may not have to buy additional needles right away. However, most pro turntables only include the headshells to mount the needles on and the actual cartridges are sold separately.

Slipmats

Slipmat

Slipmats are thin felt discs that fit on the platter underneath the record. They protect your records and allow the platter to spin freely while you touch the vinyl. Thicker mats provide more insulation against possible feedback caused by bass vibrations while thinner mats create more of a slippery feel for scratching and tricks.

TIP: If your turntable comes with a rubber mat, toss it before putting on your slipmat. You'll go crazy trying to mix with it on!

CD PLAYERS

You can either get a dual CD player with two players in one unit, or you can opt for the stand-alone single-CD decks, which act more like turntables. We are going to focus on the single-CD decks because they give you more freedom in your performance. However, all these techniques can also be applied to the dual players.

The industry standard CD turntables are Pioneer CDJs, although there are many manufacturers that make quality CD decks. The options vary on all of them, but in addition to great sound quality, the main features to look for are:

» **Reaction time**. PLAY/PAUSE button with an instant start/stop (no-latency).

» **Vinyl mode**. Manipulate CDs as if they were records.

» **Large jog wheel**. Easier control (6+ inches is best, especially for scratching).

» **Digital display**. Large and comprehensive.

» **Cue points**. Ability to set and save them.

» **Key lock**. Stabilizes the key, regardless of how fast or slow the song is playing.

» **Responsive pitch control**. Fast, dependable speed adjustments.

A CD turntable and its essential features:

1 CUE: Sets and triggers cue points

2 DIGITAL DISPLAY: Displays sound wave, BPM, track info, tempo, effects, and looping settings

3 DISC LOADING SLOT: CD goes here

4 EJECT: Removes CD

5 JOG DIAL DISPLAY: Indicates cue point position and vinyl mode display

6 JOG MODE SELECT (VINYL/ CDJ): Toggles between VINYL and CDJ mode

7 JOG WHEEL: Allows you to control the CD manually as if it were a vinyl record

8 MASTER TEMPO BUTTON (KEY LOCK): Locks the song's key so if you speed up/slow down the tempo using the pitch control the key won't change.

9 PLAY/PAUSE: Starts and stops the CD

10 POWER SWITCH: Turns it on

11 SEARCH BUTTONS: Fast forward or rewind the song with these buttons

12 TEMPO CONTROL KNOB (PITCH CONTROL): Changes playing speed of the CD. Faster is "+", Slower is "-".

Pioneer
CDJ-2000
Diagram

13 TEMPO CONTROL RANGE: Changes range of the pitch control so that you can go farther with speed changes (±6, ±10, ±16, ±100)

14 TEMPO RESET: Resets tempo to "0" regardless of pitch control's position

15 TIME MODE / AUTO CUE: Changes display mode to show either the song's remaining time or elapsed time. Also toggles between Auto Cue on and off. When Auto cue is on it sets a cue point before each song and automatically stops the CD between each song.

16 TRACK SEARCH BUTTONS: Skips to next track or previous track.

17 VINYL SPEED ADJUST RELEASE/ START DIAL: Adjusts how fast/ slow the song starts after you take your hand off the jog wheel

18 VINYL SPEED ADJUST TOUCH/ BRAKE DIAL: Adjusts how fast/ slow the song stops after you take your hand off the jog wheel

MIXERS

If you use turntables, CDs, or Serato Scratch Live, you're definitely going to need a DJ mixer. If you use a DJ software program offering an internal virtual DJ mixer or a DJ controller incorporating a mixer within its hardware, you won't need to buy an extra mixer. However, these designs are based on a traditional DJ mixer, so you should understand its basic functions.

DJ mixers come in all shapes, sizes, and price ranges. The good news is you don't have to spend a fortune to get something decent to learn on. You can save money in this department now and then invest in something more substantial later when you're ready to spend the extra cash.

As far as features go, DJ mixers can range from very basic to completely tricked out with complex functions, so shop around to see what's available. Bells and whistles aside, the basic functions to look for are:

» **Two channels**. So you can mix one song into another. Get more channels if you want to mix more than two sources.

» **Crossfader with a curve adjustment**. Adjusts the fade settings from sharp to smooth. (This is essential if you want to scratch).

» **Decent sound quality**. Be aware that the more expensive mixers usually offer better preamps for better sound quality, but as long as it sounds decent you're cool for now.

A two-channel DJ mixer and its basic functions:

Rane
TTM-56
Mixer

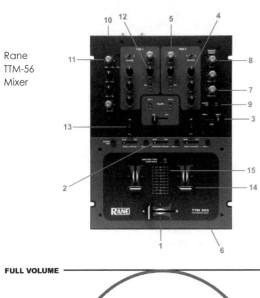

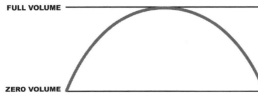

Crossfader Curve Adjustment: Slow Fade

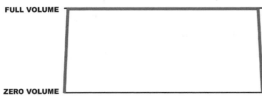

Crossfader Curve Adjustment: Fast Cut

1 CROSSFADER: Cuts or fades from one channel to the other. Push it all the way to the left; you only hear the left deck. Push it all the way to the right; you only hear the right deck. In the middle you hear both.

2 CROSSFADER CURVE ADJUSTMENT: Adjusts the fade of the crossfader from really a smooth fading transition to a quick cut transition. When set to smooth, the volume starts from zero on the left and right sides and gradually fades up to the loudest point when the fader hits the middle point, cross fading between the two channels. When set to sharp cut, the sound hits to full volume immediately when the fader leaves the left or right side. The tighter the cut, the better it is for scratching.

3 CUE PAN: Crossfades from one channel to the other in your headphones. Push it all the way to the left; you only hear the left deck. Push it all the way to the right; you only hear the right deck. In the middle you hear both. Use this to hear only one track, listen to one louder than the other or preview both at the same volume.

4 EQ (HI, MID, LOW): Volume knobs for the 3 main frequencies. Hi adjusts the track's highs (Treble), Mid adjusts the midrange, and Low adjusts the deepest frequencies (Bass). The best mixers have complete kill to zero, meaning when the knob is all the way down you don't hear anything at all from that frequency. Test this by playing a song and turning all the knobs to zero. If you hear sound it doesn't have complete kill.

5 GAIN: Master volume knobs for each channel. Once your song's volume fader is up, if it's still too quiet, boost its volume using the gain.

6 HEADPHONE JACK: Plug in headphones here.

7 HEADPHONE VOLUME: Adjusts the volume in your headphones.

8 MASTER VOLUME: Overall volume for entire mixer.

9 MASTER/CUE: Switches between Master (dancefloor audio) and Cue (your own private domain) in your headphones.

10 MIC INPUT: Plug in mic here.

11 MIC VOLUME: Adjusts mic volume.

12 PAN: Moves the sound all the way to the left speaker or the right speaker.

13 PHONO/LINE SWITCH: Switches channel between Phono and Line Input. Phono is for turntables. Line is for digital (CD, Serato Scratch Live etc)

14 VOLUME FADERS: Fades channel's volume in and out.

15 VOLUME METERS: Visually displays track's volume.

DJ SOFTWARE

DJ software is used to play digital audio files and there are many different options available. Some programs require external hardware such as turntables, CDJs, and mixers or All-In-One DJ Midi Controllers, while others are completely internal. Features range drastically and technology moves so fast that by the time this book is published there might be a ton of new functions offered in each program. So for this book we're just going to concentrate on the main features to look out for. Not all of them are necessary for DJing but if you're going to use software, you might as well get something that you can grow into.

» **Library organization.** Intuitive, user-friendly method of organizing song files and DJ sets. This is essential to quickly and easily find what song to play next.

» **Effects.** Audio effects such as echoes, flangers, phasers, and filters.

» **Looping.** Loops audio.

» **Sampler.** Stores and triggers samples.

» **Cue points.** Sets visual cue points in songs.

» **Comments.** Lets you write text on your song files and saves the info on the ID3 tags.

» **Search.** Uses keywords to help you find songs in your audio library.

» **Sort.** Organizes a selection of tracks by beats per minute (bpm), key, artist name, track name, and so on.

» **Analog-to-digital converter.** Hardware box with RCA and USB ports used to connect a laptop to the mixer and turntables or CD players.

» **Internal mixer.** Optional virtual DJ mixer within software.

» **Video capabilities.** Ability to mix video (with or without audio).

» **MIDI control.** Ability to control software functions.

» **Internal decks.** User-friendly virtual turntables.

» **Sound wave display.** Various programs display audio differently. Some offer multiple options for viewing, including lining up sound waves visually to help with beat matching.

» **BPM counter.** Counts the beats per minute.

» **Key lock.** Stabilizes the song's key so it doesn't change when you speed up or slow down the tempo.

» **Auto sync.** Matches the song's tempos. (But you won't need this feature because you're going to learn how to match your own beats with this book!)

Serato Scratch Live   Traktor Scratch

DJ MIDI CONTROLLERS

DJ MIDI controllers are used to manipulate DJ software, just like their traditional counterparts. Many are all-in-one controllers that offer the entire audio player/ mixer setup in one unit, yet are smaller and more compact so they are much easier to travel with than decks and a mixer. They are modeled after the traditional gear, so all the core functions mimic the functions of a mixer and turntables/CDJs setup. All the techniques taught in this book can also be applied to these types of controllers. If you are interested in using an all-in-one DJ MIDI controller, here are some of the main features you'll want to look for:

» **Size and Durability.** If you want to travel with a controller, it has to be a manageable size and made well so that it can take the bumps and bruises of being on the road. If you don't plan to move it around much, then you may want to check out a bigger unit that will give you a more traditional gear experience.

» **Jog Wheels.** These are a must if you want to manipulate your songs as if they were playing on records or CDs. Jog wheels give you more functionality than buttons and knobs alone. At least five to six inches or more in diameter is best if you want to get into scratching and turntablist tricks.

» **Buttons and Knobs.** Some controllers offer more functionality than others, so make sure it has enough buttons and knobs to control your software as you'd like to.

» **Software.** All controllers cater to at least one specific type of software and usually come bundled with it in the package. Make sure you research various types of software and decide what you need so you know what you are getting with each controller.

» **Versatility.** Some controllers will work with more than one type of software, allowing you to "map" their controls manually via MIDI. This is a cool feature if you want the freedom to work with multiple platforms. However, if you prefer one type of software, then it's best to just get a controller that is built for that specific software because it will have all the functions you need already set up for you.

» **Inputs and Outputs.** If you want to hook up additional gear, you will need a controller with extra input and output jacks.

» **Sound Card.** The sound card enables you to preview songs in your headphones and have music playing out of the main speakers at the same time. It also allows you to incorporate external decks, mics, and recording outputs. Many controllers come with a sound card built in. However, some don't, so you may have to buy one separately, adding to the overall cost.

Vestax VCI-300 MK2 DJ Controller

NI Traktor Kontrol S4 DJ Controller

TIP: Check out www.digitaldjtips.com for cool buying guides and additional advice on portable digital DJ gear!

WHERE TO SHOP

You know what you need, now it's time to go shopping!

DJ EQUIPMENT

Awesome deals are usually found online. You can easily compare prices, read customer reviews, and in addition many sites offer free shipping. Before surfing the web, visit a physical store to try different gear and decide what's best for you.

If you buy from a physical store, you'll have the advantage of testing out the gear and asking a salesperson questions. For example, you should ask if extra wires or anything else is needed for your setup.

Buying used gear is also an option both online and off. You should test it to make sure everything works correctly. If purchased online without testing, make sure that the seller offers full refunds for returns. Some physical stores also offer used gear.

MUSIC
This depends on what genres you want to play and what media you're using.

Vinyl Records and CDs
An online search is an easy way to find music websites and local record shops catering to your genre. Online shops usually have a huge selection and you can compare prices. Physical stores sometimes allow you to listen to the exact item you are buying so you can check for any scratches or defects. Buying used is a great way to find older stuff that is out of print. eBay and Craigslist have tons of people selling used records and CDs, sometimes entire collections. Many physical music stores have bulletin areas where people post flyers if they're selling records or announcing swap meets and record shows. Yard sales and thrift stores are awesome places to find used records and CDs on the cheap.

Digital Audio
Ahhhh, the Internet. Instant gratification!

There are lots of places to download music online. Just search for five seconds and you're bound to find what you're looking for. In addition to buying from online stores, you can find many places to legally download music for free; you just have to do a little digging. Many artists and producers offer free downloads on their websites and on social media profiles such as Facebook and SoundCloud. There are lots of music blogs that legally offer free downloads as well.

(Notice I said legally. Please support the artists and don't steal their music. The legit downloads usually sound better anyway, and you won't risk downloading a virus, otherwise known as instant karma! Okay, I'm jumping off the soapbox now.)

Here's a listing of music websites to get you started:

» www.beatport.com: electronic dance music (digital)

» www.amazon.com: all genres (digital, vinyl, CDs)

» www.itunes.com: hip-hop, electronic dance music (digital)

» www.trackitdown.net: electronic dance music (digital)

» www.turntablelab.com: all genres (digital, vinyl, CDs)

» www.juno.co.uk: electronic dance music (digital, vinyl, CDs)

» www.djcity.com: hip-hop, scratch (vinyl)

» www.ebay.com: all genres (vinyl, CDs)

» www.craigslist.com: all genres (vinyl, CDs)

» www.ameobamusic.com: all genres (vinyl, CDs)

» www.satelliterecords.com: electronic dance music (digital)

» www.fye.com: all genres (CDs)

» www.soundcloud.com: all genres. A social media–based website where artists promote their music by posting it for free download or for preview with links to buy (digital).

» www.dubstep.net: dubstep and drumstep—free downloads (digital)

TOP LEFT: Beatport
TOP RIGHT: TrackItDown
LEFT: SoundCloud

Facebook Free
Downloads
on Artist Pages

HOOK IT UP!

Okay, you spent a ton of cash on your gear, so don't just let it sit there—hook
it up!

First unpack, position everything in place, and leave the power off. Keep
the manuals handy. (Reading them is also a good idea!)

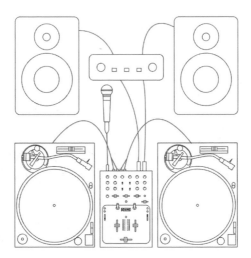

Full Set Up

TURNTABLES

Fasten the thin ground wires to the back of the mixer,
set the phono/line switch to "phono," and plug the
RCA connectors into the phono inputs for each
channel. On a two-channel mixer, the left turntable
plugs into the phono inputs of channel 1 (left side)
and the right turntable into channel 2 (right side).

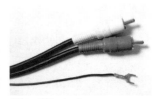

RCAs / Grounds

CD PLAYERS

Plug the RCA connectors into the line inputs on the mixer and set the phono/line switch to "line." On a two-channel mixer, the left turntable plugs into the phono inputs of channel 1 (left side) and the right turntable into channel 2 (right side).

Back of Mixer

MIXER

The master output connects to your amp, stereo system, or self-powered speakers. You may need to get an extra wire for this. If so check the mixer outputs and speaker system inputs and get wires that have the correct connectors on each end. For example, if your mixer has XLR outputs and your powered speakers have quarter-inch inputs, then you will need to get two cables with female XLRs and male quarter-inch inputs, one for each speaker.

SOFTWARE

Install the software on your computer according to the manual. Plug the turntable's (or CD player's) RCA cables into the input jacks for the left and right decks on the converter box that came with the software. Plug one end of the (included) RCA cables into the appropriate RCA output jacks on the converter box. Plug the other end of the RCA cables into your mixer's appropriate RCA input jacks for the right and left decks. Plug one end of the USB cable into the converter box and the

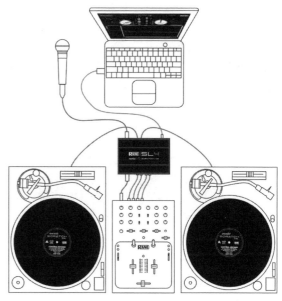

Laptop Set Up

other end into your computer's USB jack. If you are using an All-In-One DJ controller such as the Native Instruments Traktor Kontroller S4m, then simply plug it directly into your laptop using the USB cable. Launch the software and adjust the settings according to the software manual. Import your music according to the directions and test it out using the control vinyl/CDs or midi controller that came with your software package.

Serato Converter Box

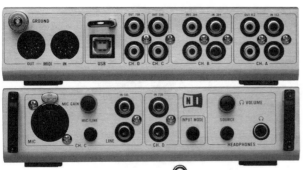

Traktor Converter Box

Part 2 GETTING BUSY

3 IS THIS THING ON?

Now that your gear is all hooked up and ready to go, let's fire it up!

MIXER

Before you turn everything on, make sure all the volume faders are down. When playing audio for the first time, it's best to start from zero and gradually fade up, just to be safe.

EXERCISE 1: MIXER

1. Turn on mixer.
2. Plug in headphones.
3. Set headphones setting to "cue" and set the cue fader (or knob) so that both the left and right decks will play in the headphones.
4. Check the master, gain, and headphone volume levels to make sure they aren't turned up too high. It's always best to start at a lower volume rather than risk blasting your speakers or your ears by mistake because you had it maxed from the start.
5. Set the crossfader in the middle and the volume faders down so that no sound will be heard from the speakers yet.
6. Start playing music on the right deck (see the following directions on playing music).

Volume Faders Down

7. Music should be playing in headphones. If not, make sure the right deck is set to play in the headphones and/or turn the headphone volume up a bit more.

8. Gradually slide the right volume fader up to hear the music out of the speakers. If you don't hear anything, check the gain knob for that channel and make sure it's turned up. (Gains should be set around twelve o'clock.)

Right Volume Fader Up

You should be hearing music in the speakers and headphones. If not, check to make sure everything is hooked up correctly.

TURNTABLES

Here we'll focus on the current industry standard for DJs, the Technics 1200 or 1210. There are many other options available and all have the same general features, so these directions can apply to them as well.

EXERCISE 2: PUT THE NEEDLE ON THE RECORD!

1. Turn POWER switch on.

2. Put the record on the turntable. The slipmat should be in between the record and the platter.

3. Press the START/STOP button to start rotating the platter and the record.

4. Using your thumb and pointer finger, carefully pick up the needle using the thin handle on the headshell.

5. Gently place the needle at the beginning of the record. If you're rough or careless during this step, you'll risk scratching your records with the needle, so don't just plop it down on the record. Once the grooves are scratched you can't go back!

Placing Needle on Turntable

6. The record should be playing music. If not, make sure your mixer volumes are set correctly and everything is hooked up right.

7. Press the START/STOP button to stop the record.

To return the song to the beginning, pick up the needle by the handle and gently place it back at the beginning of the record.

EXERCISE 3: HOLDING THE RECORD

1. Place your hand on the record at nine o'clock. Right hand controls the right turntable. Left hand controls the left turntable.

2. Press START/STOP and hold the record in place with your hand to keep it from spinning.

3. Don't push down too hard or you'll stop the platter from spinning. The platter should spin freely underneath.

4. To play the record, just let go!

5. To stop the record, place your hand at nine o'clock.

6. Practice holding the record and letting it go a few times to get the feel of it.

Holding the Record

EXERCISE 4: REWINDING THE RECORD

1. Press START/STOP to play the record.

2. Place your finger on the record label.

3. Push down and rotate the record counter-clockwise by turning the label in the opposite direction of record play. Don't push down too hard or you'll stop the platter underneath.

Rewinding the Record

EXERCISE 5: FORWARDING THE RECORD

1. Press START/STOP to play the record.

2. Place your finger on the record label.

3. Push down and rotate the record clockwise by turning the label in the same direction of record play. Don't push down too hard or you'll stop the platter underneath.

Forwarding the Record

TIP: Keep your hand on the record label when rewinding or forwarding; otherwise, you risk hitting the needle off the record!

EXERCISE 6: CUEING THE RECORD

Cueing means to find the starting place of your song.

1. Press START/STOP to play the record.

2. Place the needle at the beginning of the record.

3. If you don't hear sound, forward the record by turning the label with your fingers until you hear the first sound and then hold it there.

4. If you do hear sound when you first put the needle on, then rewind it with your fingers on the label until you don't hear anything, and then hold it there.

5. Step three or four should get you to the exact beginning of the song where the sound starts.

6. Carefully put your hand at nine o'clock to hold the record in place at the very beginning of the song.

7. Let the record go and let it play.

8. Rewind the record back to the beginning and practice cueing it up again.

9. If there's more than one song on the same side of the record, practice cueing up the next song farther toward the center using the same techniques. The secret is to look for the darker grooves. The darkest areas on the record have little to no sound, so this will give you a hint as to where the next song starts.

CD PLAYERS

Here we'll focus on the current industry standard, the Pioneer CDJ. There are many other options available and although certain functions and layouts may vary, most of them have the same general features, so these directions should also apply to them.

EXERCISE 7: PLAYING THE CD

1. Turn on the CDJ.

2. The auto cue/remain settings should automatically be set to on. If auto cue is turned off, hold down the TIME MODE/AUTO CUE button for a second until the auto cue light turns on.

Auto Cue

3. Insert the CD into the front slot, label side up.

4. Wait for the disc to load and the CD info to display.

5. Press the PLAY/PAUSE button to play the CD.

6. Press the PLAY/PAUSE button again to stop the CD.

7. To return to the beginning of the song, press the left TRACK SEARCH button: ◄◄

8. Push the EJECT button in the top right to eject the CD.

All Search Buttons

EXERCISE 8: REWINDING THE CD

1. Press the PLAY/PAUSE button to play the CD.

2. To rewind the song, press and hold the left SEARCH button: ◄◄

3. Let go of the button to play again.

4. You can also rewind the song by setting the jog mode to "vinyl" and rotating the jog wheel counter-clockwise to the left (just like you would a turntable).

Vinyl Mode

5. Let go of the jog wheel to play again.

6. To return to the beginning of the song, or to navigate to an earlier track, press the left TRACK SEARCH button: ◄◄

Holding Jog Wheel   Rewinding Jog Wheel

EXERCISE 9: FORWARDING THE CD

1. Press the PLAY/PAUSE button to play the CD.

2. To forward the song a little bit, press and hold the right SEARCH button: ►►

3. Let go of the button to play again.

4. You can also forward the song by setting the jog mode to "vinyl" and rotating the jog wheel clockwise to the right (just like you would a turntable).

5. Let go of the jog wheel to play again.

6. To skip to the beginning of the next track, press the right TRACK SEARCH button: ▶▶|

Forwarding Jog Wheel

EXERCISE 10: CUEING THE CD

"Cueing" means to find the starting place of your song.

1. Insert the CD.

2. Navigate to the song you want to play by using the TRACK SEARCH buttons: ▶▶| or |◀◀

3. Press PLAY/PAUSE to play from the beginning of the track.

4. To start the track at a different place other than the beginning of the song, use the SEARCH buttons while the CDJ is set to pause.

5. Press PLAY to play from that spot.

6. You can also forward or rewind the song by setting the jog mode to "vinyl," rotating the jog wheel, and holding the song in place with your hand once you locate your starting point.

7. Let go of the jog wheel to start it at that point (or) press PLAY/PAUSE to pause it and then press PLAY from that spot.

EXERCISE 11: SETTING AND ADJUSTING CUE POINTS IN CDJ MODE

You can set specific cue points to start your CD from a precise point. To jump to that point, press cue.

1. Insert the CD and press PLAY.

2. Press PLAY/PAUSE to pause the CD at the point where you want to start the CD.

3. Use the jog wheel or the SEARCH buttons to make additional adjustments to get the CD to the exact point by listening to the sound while moving the jog wheel back and forth the across the point, then pull the jog wheel back to right before the sound starts.

4. Press the CUE button to save the current cue point in the memory and erase the previous one.

5. To adjust this cue point, press the CUE button while the CD is playing to jump to that cue point.

6. Press either SEARCH button to set to audible pause mode and repeat steps three and four.

Cue Button

EXERCISE 12: SETTING AND ADJUSTING CUE POINTS IN VINYL MODE

You can set specific cue points to start your CD from a precise point. To jump to that point, press cue.

1. Insert the CD and press PLAY.

2. Activate the jog wheel by pressing the jog mode SELECT button and selecting "vinyl" mode. Once vinyl mode is set, the CDJ will remember the setting even when it's turned off so you won't have to do it again.

3. Press PLAY/PAUSE or press and hold the top of the jog wheel to pause the CD where you want to start.

4. Turn back the jog wheel to right before the cue point sound starts.

5. While holding the jog wheel in place, press the CUE button to save the current cue point in the memory and erase the previous one.

6. To adjust this cue point, press the CUE button while the CD is playing to jump to that cue point.

7. Press either SEARCH button to set to audible pause mode and repeat steps three, four, and five.

SOFTWARE AND ALL-IN-ONE CONTROLLERS

If you're using turntables or CD players to control DJ software such as Serato Scratch Live or Traktor Scratch Pro, most of the same hardware rules apply. However, since the audio is coming from your computer instead of a record or CD, it changes things just a bit. Instead of choosing your track using search buttons or a turntable needle, you'll select the tune within your software, and then map it onto the deck by either dragging the song file to the virtual deck or using a keyboard shortcut. After that, everything is pretty much the same as far as hardware control goes.

Most virtual DJ instruments are inspired by the hardware, so the internal players and mixers usually follow the same protocol as far as playing, rewinding, forwarding, and so on. For example, Serato Scratch Live offers internal decks that have similar features of real decks. Traktor Scratch Pro offers an internal mixer that mimics a hardware mixer.

Hardware controllers used to manipulate DJ software, such as the Vestax VCI-300 to control Serato's ITCH, mimic traditional hardware as well.

I know I sound like a broken record (pun intended), but when in doubt, read the manual … it helps *a lot.*

HOW TO LISTEN

You have to get used to listening to two things at once, so learning how to listen to your music in your headphones at the same time as the monitor is essential.

» **Monitor Speakers.** Speakers in the DJ booth that allow you to hear exactly what the dance floor is hearing. Usually hooked into the mixer's booth outputs, they give you the same audio as the master out with independent volume control.

Ideally you should have volume control using the booth setting (or aux out) on your mixer, but sometimes the club hooks them into their mixing board. In this case, you have to tell the sound person controlling the volume how loud you want your monitors; otherwise, they could be too quiet, or worse they might blow your ears off.

If you're at home, then you can monitor from your main speakers. In a club, the DJ booth is usually separated from the dance floor, so you'll need monitors to hear what's going on.

» **Headphone Master/Cue.** The headphone settings on the mixer let you listen to either the *master* (what's on the dance floor) or the *cue* (your own private domain). The "cue" setting is used to get the next song ready in the headphones while the dance floor only hears the song you're playing through the master out.

Headphone Master/Cue

There are a few ways to listen and each will help you in different situations, so practice them all. You'll also find that you may combine techniques depending on where you are in your mix.

HEADPHONES WITH MONITOR

This means you're listening to the monitor with one ear and listening to the headphones with the other. The monitor always plays the master (dance floor audio); however, the headphones offer more options. In the headphone ear, you can isolate one deck, listen to both decks, or listen to the master.

EXERCISE 13: HEADPHONE/MONITOR MIX

1. Put a song on each deck and press PLAY on both.

2. Push the crossfader all the way to the left.

3. Put your headphones on with one earphone on one ear and slide the other earphone off the other ear, leaving it open to listen to the monitor.

One Earphone Off

4. Set your mixer's headphone MASTER/CUE setting to "cue."

5. Adjust the headphone cue fader (or knob) to play only the right deck.

6. You should hear the left deck in the speakers (dance floor audio) and the right deck in the headphones (cue).

7. Now adjust the headphone cue fader to listen to both decks in the headphones at the same volume.

8. You should hear the left deck in the speakers (dance floor audio) and both decks in the headphones (cue).

9. Experiment with this setting to make one deck louder than the other and vice versa. This trick helps when you want to hear both in the headphones but need to accentuate the volume of one so it stands out more than the other.

10. Now set your mixer's headphone MASTER/CUE setting to "master."

11. You should hear the left deck in the speakers and the headphones (dance floor audio). You'd use this setting if you only want to hear the master out, usually when the volume of both songs are up and the mix becomes audible on the dance floor.

ALL IN THE HEADPHONES

This is exactly what it sounds like: you're mixing totally in the headphones. It's the most accurate way of listening because everything is of equal distance from your ears, so there is no delay or outside noise to get in the way. It's also an important skill to learn because it will save your butt in sketchy situations where you have a hard time hearing the monitor.

For example, the monitor may be crappy, shorting out, broken, or just plain not there (not cool!).

Sometimes there's a delay between the monitor and the headphones because it's too far away from you, making it really difficult to mix.

Or the club's sound system may be too loud, overpowering the monitor and making it impossible to hear.

In fact, sometimes the club is so crazy loud that you literally need to shield your ears! (I also recommend using custom-fitted musician earplugs to protect your hearing.)

Regardless of the reason, mixing in the headphones is a must-have skill. Just be sure to always check in with the outside world after every mix to make sure things are running smoothly on the dance floor. You don't want to perform the best mix of your life, only to find out that the master volume was down and nobody heard it but you!

EXERCISE 14: HEADPHONE MIX

1. Put a song on each deck and press PLAY on both.

2. Push the crossfader all the way to the left.

3. Listen to both of your headphones at the same time, one with each ear.

4. Set your mixer's headphone MASTER/CUE setting to "cue."

5. Adjust the headphone cue fader (or knob) to play only the right deck. This would be the song you are preparing to bring in.

6. Now adjust the headphone cue fader (or knob) to listen to both decks in the headphones at the same volume.

7. Experiment with this setting to make one deck louder than the other and vice versa. This trick helps when you want to hear both in the headphones but need to accentuate the volume of one so it stands out more than the other in your ears. For example, if the cue pan setting is adjusted with a crossfader, slide the crossfader slightly off center so one song is louder than the other.

8. Now set your mixer's headphone MASTER/ CUE setting to "master."

9. You should be hearing the left deck in your headphones (dance floor audio). Use this setting to check back and forth between master and cue often during your mix, and also when both songs are up at full volume and the mix become audible on the dance floor.

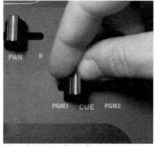
Headphone Pan Fader

10. Take one headphone off to check that the correct audio is playing out of the speakers. (In this case, it's only the left deck.)

TIP: Mixing in the headphones is awesome for practicing at home if you don't have any speakers or if you just don't want others to hear you!

SPLIT CUE

Some mixers offer a split cue feature, allowing you to hear one channel in the left earphone and the other in the right earphone. Some DJs, especially beginners, find this helpful because it literally separates the songs in your head rather then combining them in both ears at the same time. If you don't have this feature, don't worry because you'll naturally tune your ears to decipher which song is which through practice. You can also mimic this feature by using the headphone/monitor method discussed earlier.

4 BREAKING DOWN THE MUSIC

In order to spin it, you have to understand what's in it!

BEAT

The beat is the rhythm in a song that you nod your head to.

EXERCISE 15: FIND THE BEAT!

1. Play a song.
2. Nod your head to the main driving rhythm. The beats should seem to repeat one after the other with equal space between them.
3. Now listen to another song and repeat step two. Easy!

DRUMS

Drums are the most important sounds to listen for because they keep the beat. Tuning your ears to the different drum sounds in the music will help you to match the beats of two songs together.

> » **Kick Drum** (**Bass Drum**). The lowest-sounding drum in the kit. In house, techno, and trance music, it's the drum that sounds like "thump, thump, thump, thump" and it usually repeats on every beat: "1, 2, 3, 4." In hip-hop, breakbeat, and rock music, it generally falls on beats one and three in each bar: "1, —, 3, —."

Bass Drum

(Don't worry, you'll learn how to count beats and bars in the next section.)

» **Snare Drum.** The higher pitched, snappy-sounding drum that usually falls on the second and fourth beat of the bar: "—, 2, —, 4."

Snare Drum

» **Hi-Hat.** Two cymbals that clasp together and then are hit with a drumstick. It usually sounds like "tss, tss, tss, tss" and can sometimes hit on the main beats as well as between the beats: "1, &, 2, &, 3, &, 4, &."

» **Percussion.** Additional drums or other rhythmic instruments helping to keep the beat, such as congas, bongos, tom-toms, tambourines, shakers, cowbells, triangles, and hand claps.

Hi-Hat

EXERCISE 16: IDENTIFYING THE MAIN DRUM KIT!

1. Play a song.

2. Set your mixer's EQ so that all the EQ knobs are pointed straight up in the middle at twelve o'clock.

3. Emphasize the kick drum sound by turning the high and middle EQs all the way down to zero counter-clockwise. This isolates the bass frequencies so that you can really hear the kick drum.

EQ Twelve O'clock   EQ Bass Emphasis

4. Turn the high- and mid-range EQ back to twelve o'clock, and then turn the low EQ all the way down counter-clockwise to emphasize the snare drum sound.

5. Leaving the low EQ down, turn the mid-range EQ all the way down counter-clockwise to isolate the hi-hat sounds.

EQ Snare Emphasis   EQ Hi-Hat Emphasis

6. Turn the low- and mid-range EQ back to twelve o'clock.

7. Listen for the thumping kick drum and clap your hands when it hits.

8. Listen for the snare and clap when it hits.

9. Listen for the hi-hat and clap when it hits. You just tuned your ears to the drums!

COUNTING MUSIC

You have to understand a little about how music is written so you can count it correctly and mix your songs in the right places. Don't worry; it's as easy as 1, 2, 3, 4!

BARS

A bar (or "measure") is made up of a group of beats that you count so you know where you are in the music. What does a bar actually look like and how do you know how many beats to count in a group? Check it out. . . .

Music Staff Diagram

Music is written out on a series of horizontal lines called a *staff.*

A vertical line drawn through the staff is called a *bar line.*

The *bar* is the space between two bar lines where the beats are grouped together.

Notes are symbols that show how long a sound lasts. There are different kinds of notes and they all relate to each other mathematically. The longest-sounding note is the *whole note*. It lasts four beats and you can only have one whole note in a bar.

NOTE VALUES

Notes That Fit in One 4/4 Bar

1 whole note is equal to

2 half notes

4 quarter notes

8 eighth notes

16 sixteenth notes

4/4 Time Signature

A little fraction code at the beginning of the staff called the *time signature* tells you how to count the beats. Most of the music DJs play is in 4/4 time, which means there are four beats in every bar.

The top number represents the number of beats to count in each bar: four beats.

The bottom number indicates which type of note receives one beat (or count): the quarter note.

TIP: A bar of 4/4 time is like a dollar bill. One dollar (whole note) is equal to four twenty-five-cent quarters (quarter notes).

Since one bar is four beats, we count it: "1, 2, 3, 4."

Four Bars of Four Beats

To keep track of the bars as we go along, we count them: "1, 2, 3, 4 | 2, 2, 3, 4 | 3, 2, 3, 4 | 4, 2, 3, 4," and so on.

EXERCISE 17: COUNT THE BARS!

1. Play a song.

2. Count the bars from the very first beat. Do this by counting "1, 2, 3, 4 | 2, 2, 3, 4 | 3, 2, 3, 4 | 4, 2, 3, 4," and so on. Go as far as you can until you get used to it.

3. Play another song that's faster or slower and count the bars from the beginning.

4. Count the bars of songs in different genres.

PHRASES

A phrase is a group of bars. The amount of bars in each phrase varies, depending on what part of the song it is and what genre of music it is.

In hip-hop, rock, pop, and other vocal-based music, the phrases are generally two, four, eight, or sixteen bars long.

In electronic dance music, such as house, techno, trance, drum

Eight-Bar Phrase with the "One"

and bass, and dubstep, phrases are generally a bit longer with eight, sixteen, thirty-two, or sixty-four bars.

TIP: Think of a phrase as a sentence. The beats are the letters and the bars are the words that make up that sentence.

THE "ONE"

The "one" is the first beat in the phrase. This is the beat that you want to drop your next song in on.

Most songs give you a musical clue as to where the beginning of the phrase is by bringing in a new recurring sound like a new cymbal pattern, guitar riff, or vocals. For example, in electronic dance music, you'll usually hear a little clue (i.e., extra drum fill) every four bars, then a bigger clue (i.e., cymbal crash) every eight bars, and then a huge clue (i.e., a new melodic instrument, drum roll, or big cymbal crash) every sixteen or thirty-two bars.

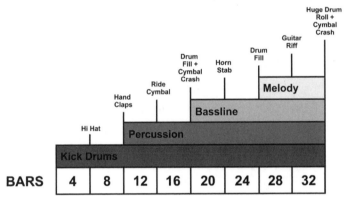

Phrases with Clues

When you first start out, you may have to count every bar in every phrase to know where you are in the song. However, over time and with the help of the musical clues, you'll be able to "feel" the phrases and instinctively know where the "one" is in each phrase without having to count.

EXERCISE 18: COUNT PHRASES AND IDENTIFY THE "ONES"!

1. Play a song.

2. Count the bars in four-bar phrases from the very first beat and then repeat a few times: "1, 2, 3, 4 | 2, 2, 3, 4 | 3, 2, 3, 4 | 4, 2, 3, 4, | 1, 2, 3, 4 | 2, 2, 3, 4 | 3, 2, 3, 4 | 4, 2, 3, 4," and so on. Every time you repeat, you're identifying the "one" of that four-bar phrase!

3. Count the bars in eight-bar phrases from the very first beat and then repeat a few times: 1, 2, 3, 4 | 2, 2, 3, 4 | 3, 2, 3, 4 | 4, 2, 3, 4 | 5, 2, 3, 4 | 6, 2, 3, 4 | 7, 2, 3, 4 | 8, 2, 3, 4 | 1, 2, 3, 4 | 2, 2, 3, 4..."

4. Try counting longer phrases of sixteen and thirty-two bars.

5. In hip-hop, rock, or pop (vocal songs): listen for musical clues at the beginning of each four-bar phrase, eight-bar phrase, and sixteen-bar phrase.

6. In electronic dance music (house, techno, drum and bass, dubstep, trance. etc.): listen for musical clues at the beginning of each four-bar phrase, eight-bar phrase, sixteen-bar phrase, and thirty-two bar phrase.

SONG STRUCTURE

Phrases are grouped into different segments that make up a song.

VOCAL MUSIC (HIP-HOP, ROCK, POP, REGGAE)

» **Intro.** The beginning segment of the song. Usually this is the part used to mix into another song. If there are vocals in it, they usually introduce the song. The best intros for DJing are vocal-free. Intros usually range from two to sixteen bars, but can also be less than a beat!

» **Verse.** This is the part of the song where the vocalist tells the story. Typically you don't want to mix your next song out of a verse because the audience will be expecting the chorus to come next and you'll be cutting it short without playing the part they know best. Verses are usually sixteen bars.

» **Chorus.** The chorus, or "the hook," is the most popular part because it repeats throughout the song. It may also say the title in it. You can mix your next song out of a chorus. Choruses typically range from four to sixteen bars.

» **Bridge.** The bridge is that mysterious part of the song that's not quite a chorus and not exactly a verse. It's an extra phrase thrown in between two parts that connects, or "bridges," them together. A bridge usually follows a chorus and is also a possible mix point.

» **Outro.** The end segment of the song. A good mix point if you want to play the whole song. Outros usually range from four to sixteen bars; however, some songs don't even have them!

VOCAL MUSIC STRUCTURE

	INTRO	CHORUS	VERSE	CHORUS	VERSE	CHORUS	BRIDGE	VERSE	CHORUS	OUTRO
BARS	8	8	16	8	16	8	8	16	8	8

Vocal Song Structure Example

ELECTRONIC DANCE MUSIC (HOUSE, TECHNO, TRANCE, DRUM AND BASS, DUBSTEP, BREAKBEAT)

» **Intro.** The beginning segment of the song. Usually this is the part used to mix into another song. Dance music is much more DJ friendly than vocal-based music, offering longer segments for mixing, and the sounds often build up gradually for a more seamless mix. Intros usually range from eight to thirty-two bars.

» **Breakdown.** A part of the song where the sounds literally break down, sometimes to just one or two sounds, or even silence. The breakdown creates a break in the music so that when the song comes back in it has more impact. It's often paired with a buildup, and together the phrasing usually ranges from sixteen to thirty-two bars.

» **Buildup.** A buildup typically follows a breakdown. It's where the sounds build onto one another and usually contains a big progressive drum roll at the end, leading into the drop.

» **Drop.** This is where the main part of the song starts with the bass line and melody. There can be a few different drops in the song. Typically the intro will either lead straight into the first drop or lead into a breakdown and buildup followed by the first drop. The length of the main part of the song that follows the drop varies, but often ranges from thirty-two to sixty-four bars before the next breakdown and buildup.

» **Outro.** The end segment of the song and also usually very DJ friendly. It's made to be mixed out of because the sounds are usually breaking down gradually, which makes for a seamless mix.

DANCE MUSIC STRUCTURE

	INTRO	BREAKDOWN + BUILD	DROP	BREAKDOWN + BUILD	DROP	OUTRO
BARS	32	16	64	32	64	32

Dance Music Song Structure Example

TIP: As you get more advanced, try mixing during the various segments to experiment with different ways of combining your dance music! You have more freedom with dance music mix points than with vocal-based music, because even if there are vocals, there usually isn't the same type of chorus-verse structure.

BPM

The beats per minute, or bpm, is the amount of beats that happen within a minute. It indicates how fast or slow the song is. You can determine the bpm by using DJ software or counting manually. Once you figure it out, be sure to write it down!

EXERCISE 19: COUNTING THE BPM

You'll need a clock and a few different tunes at different speeds.

1. Set the deck's pitch control to the zero point. If it's a turntable, it should light up green in the middle.

2. Start playing a song and nodding your head to the beat.

3. Keep an eye on the clock.

4. Once the clock hits the beginning of the next minute, start counting the beats consecutively: 1, 2, 3, 4, 5, 6, 7, 8, 9, 10, 11, and so on.

5. Continue counting for the entire minute.

6. The number you end up with at the end of the minute is the bpm!

7. Write this number down on the record sleeve, CD, or MP3 file comments area because you'll need it later!

8. Repeat the entire exercise and practice counting the bpm with different songs of varying tempos.

TIP: Use a pen and paper to make marks for each beat so you don't loose count. When the minute ends, count all the marks.

Once you know the bpm, it's much easier to figure out what songs can beatmatch with each other and what songs are out of range because their tempos are too far apart. Remember, a pitch control is limited to how far it can alter the speed of your song, depending on its range. The longer the pitch control's range, the more options you'll have to match bpm that are further apart.

It's a good idea to keep any tunes you are mixing within a certain bpm range based on your pitch control's range. A safe bet is no more than five bpm apart when confined to a +8/-8 pitch control. Further then that is possible, but if your turntable doesn't have a key lock to stabilize the tone, then the music starts to sound strange the faster (or slower) it goes, especially if it contains vocals. Speed up a vocal track too much and it turns into Alvin and the Chipmunks; slow it down too much and you're treading in Barry White territory!

That said, rules are made to be broken and ultimately you're in control, so if you think it sounds good, go for it!

Here are some examples of bpm that may or may not work based on this +8/-8 scenario:

+8/-8 Pitch Range

125 and 127 = safe!

110 and 114 = safe!

96 and 101 = a bit far, but still might work

77 and 82 = far but maybe

90 and 130 = not going to happen

150 and 180 = impossible

88 and 125 = not unless hell freezes over

TIP: Exception to the rule: If the bpm of one song is close to half of another's bpm, it can work! You're basically matching one as half time and the other as double time.

70 and 140 = safe!
(70 + 70 = 140) They are essentially the same bpm!
90 and 176 = safe!
(90 + 90 = 180) 180 is only 4 bpm away from 176!

TIP: If you set your pitch control to a wider range, you'll have more options of matching bpm that are further apart. However, the wider the range, the harder it is to beatmatch because the pitch slider's speed increments get much smaller. This makes it super touchy, so you have to be extra precise with your movements.

GENRES AND TEMPOS
Here are some popular DJ genres and their tempo ranges.

House: 124–135

Techno: 130–160

Trance: 140–160

Drum and Bass: 170–180

Dubstep: 135–145

Happy Hardcore: 160–220

Hardstyle: 145–157

Hip-Hop / R & B: 65–125

Pop/Rock/Top-40: all over the place

QUANTIZED MUSIC

Quantized music is produced on a perfect time grid, so the beat doesn't fluctuate, which makes it easier to beatmatch. Most hip-hop and electronic dance music is quantized using MIDI instruments or computers. Music that isn't quantized is very difficult to beatmatch because musicians play the instruments live and the beat fluctuates. It's possible to match these songs; however, it's a challenge to keep them on because they never lock into place. Luckily many popular live songs offer DJ-friendly versions that are quantized so they'll fall exactly on beat.

FL Studio Drum Sequencer Quantized

KEY

You may be able to beatmatch two songs, but if they sound weird together causing a sudden urge to rip your ears off, don't mix 'em! It's your instincts telling you the keys don't match and this mix isn't meant to be. (Think nails on a chalkboard, ew!) To figure out which song's go together, you have to know a little about keys. Check it. ...

CLEFS

The staff has five lines and four spaces. The clef is a symbol at the left of the staff and it tells you what each line and space means.

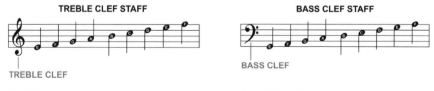

Treble Clef Staff   Bass Clef Staff

SCALES AND KEYS

In music, there are families of notes that all relate to each other called *scales*. Every scale starts with one root note that the entire scale is based on and this is called the *key*.

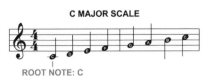
Staff with Scale of C Major and Root Note C

There are twelve possible keys a song can be written in and this comes from the twelve notes on the piano keyboard: *A, A#/Bb, B, C, C#/Db, D, D#/Eb, E, F, F#/Gb, G,* and *G#/Ab.*

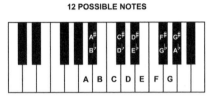
Piano Keyboard with Twelve Notes

MAJOR AND MINOR

The distance between the notes in the scale will dictate whether the key of the scale is major or minor.

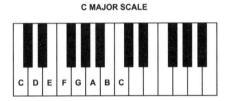

Piano Keyboard—C Major

Piano Keyboard—C-Sharp Minor

KEY SIGNATURE

This is a little code at the beginning of the staff containing symbols representing sharps (♯) and flats (♭) that tells you what key the song is in.

Staff with C-Sharp Minor Scale

HARMONIC MIXING

Mixing songs that are in key with each other is called *harmonic mixing.*

Back in the day, the only way to figure out a song's key was to find the sheet music and read its key signature, try to find a database that lists the song and its key, or just guess by playing combinations of notes on a piano while listening to the song. Regardless, you still had to have an understanding of how all the keys relate to each other in order to mix harmonically. This can get a little complicated if you don't have any background in traditional music theory. Never fear, Mixed In Key is here!

MIXED IN KEY DJ SOFTWARE

Mixed in Key scans digital music files, tells us what the keys, are and how they'll work together with other keys. (Bonus: It also counts the bpm!)

The software is based on the Camelot Wheel created by Mark Davis to help DJs learn how to mix harmonically. The Camelot Wheel is a visual representation of which keys are compatible with each other.

Each key is assigned to a key code number from one to twelve, like hours on a clock. Two songs that have the same key code will

Mixed in Key

usually mix perfectly. If you want to mix a song in a different key, the song should have a key code that falls within the hour of the first song's key code. (i.e., 12A works with 1A and 11A). This rule applies to any keys that are next to the original key you're trying to mix with (i.e., side to side or up and down, but not diagonally). For example, 3B goes with 3A, 2B, and 4B, but not 2A.

TIP: To learn more about harmonic mixing or Mixed in Key software, check out www.harmonic-mixing.com and www.mixedinkey.com

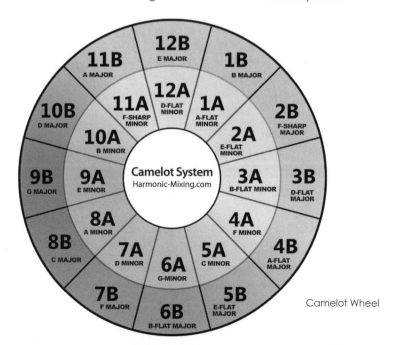

Camelot Wheel

5 DROPPING THE BEAT

Yay! It's beat dropping time! Remember how to cue up your music from chapter 3? Now you're going to drop it perfectly on beat. Pay attention because this is the most essential skill in learning how to beatmatch. The more exact you drop your beats, the easier and faster it'll be to match 'em up.

STARTER MUSIC

When you're first learning, choose instrumentals or tunes with minimal vocals. Songs with a strong distinct beat are best for learning how to beatmatch. House music is great to learn with because it has a straight kick drum hitting on all four beats in each bar. It also helps to use the same song on both decks.

BEAT DROPPING OPTIONS

If you're simply hitting play on a CD player, controller, or within a piece of software, it's all about hitting it exactly on beat, which is pretty easy. However, if you're using turntables, controlling CDJs with the jog wheel in vinyl mode, or manipulating a controller using a hands-on technique, there is a bit more to it than just pressing a button. The good news? You guys get to scratch!

BABY SCRATCH

The "baby scratch" is simply rubbing the record back and forth by hand. It's the scratch that every other scratch is based on and the foundation of dropping your beat.

EXERCISE 20: BABY SCRATCH

If using a record, you'll need a sticker.

1. Press PLAY and cue up your song to the first beat.

2. Hold your hand on the record (or jog wheel) at nine o'clock.

3. Rub the first beat back and forth a little bit to find the exact starting point of the sound.

4. If using a record, stick a little sticker on the label at twelve o'clock. This visually marks the beat's starting point. If using a controller jog wheel with dj software, look at the sound wave on the computer screen to see the beat's starting point.

Sticker

Hold at Twelve O'clock

Jog Wheel Line

5. If using a CDJ, look at the jog dial display and take note of where the line falls in the circle, marking the beat's starting point. If using a controller jog wheel with DJ software, look at the sound wave on the computer screen to see the beat's starting point.

6. Without letting go, push the record (or jog wheel) forward about an inch or two with your fingers.

Hold Jog Wheel

Baby Push Record

Baby Push Jog Wheel

7. Now pull it back to the beat's start point. (Check out the sticker, digital line, or computer's sound wave to ensure the sound is at the beginning.)

Baby Pull Record   Baby Pull Jog Wheel

8. Push it forward an inch or two.

9. Pull it back to its start point.

10. Repeat steps eight and nine until you're a baby scratch expert!

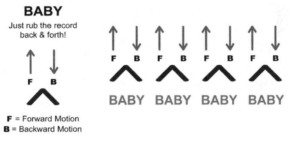

BABY

Just rub the record
back & forth!

F = Forward Motion
B = Backward Motion

Baby Scratch Symbols

RELEASE SCRATCH

The release scratch is literally just letting the record go at a specific point in the song. By now you can already do this, you just need to know how to pull it back correctly so you can let it go again!

EXERCISE 21: RELEASE SCRATCH

Record should still be marked with sticker.

1. Press PLAY and cue up the song to the first beat.

2. Hold your hand on the record (or jog wheel) at nine o'clock.

3. Rub the first beat back and forth a little bit to find the exact starting point of the sound.

4. Take a visual note of the start point using the sticker, jog wheel display, or sound wave.

5. Lift your hand up off the record (or the jog wheel).

Release Record   Release Jog Wheel

6. Let it play for about a quarter turn while following the rotation with your hand hovering over the record (or jog wheel).

Release Stop Record   Release Stop Jog Wheel   Record Release Pull

7. Stop the record (or jog wheel) by placing your hand down at twelve o'clock.

8. Pull the record (or jog wheel) back to its start point and hold.

9. Make sure the sticker, digital line, or sound wave is where it started. If done correctly, your hand should be at nine o'clock, where it began.

Jog Wheel Release Pull

10. Repeat steps five through nine until you master this.

Bonus: Try releasing the song, letting it play for four beats and rewinding it back to the start point (i.e., release, 1, 2, 3, 4, rewind to start, repeat!).

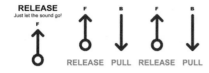

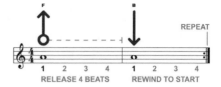

Release Scratch Symbols

Release Scratch and Play Four Beats
with Notation

BABY-RELEASE COMBO

It's time to combine the baby and release. Focus on the forward motion of the
baby scratch so that when it's time to release the record, your hand is already
moving in the forward direction. We're going to perform four baby scratches in
a bar of four beats: 1, 2, 3, 4, and then release for four beats: 1, 2, 3, 4!

EXERCISE 22: BABY, BABY, BABY, BABY, RELEASE!

The record should still be marked with the sticker.

1. Press PLAY and cue up the song to the first beat.

2. Hold your hand on the record (or jog wheel) at nine o'clock.

3. Take a visual note of the starting point using the sticker, jog wheel display,
   or sound wave.

4. Perform four baby scratches by moving the record (or jog wheel) forward
   (and back) four times on an eighth-note pattern: 1, &, 2, &, 3, &, 4, &.
   (The forward motion is always on: 1, 2, 3, 4).

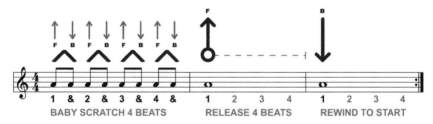

Baby, Baby, Baby, Release, and Play Four Beats Notation

5. Release the record (or jog wheel) and let it play for four beats: 1, 2, 3, 4

6. Rewind the song back to its start point.

7. Repeat steps four through six until you master this.

TIP: Baby, baby, baby, baby, release = forward + forward + forward +
forward + release!

DROPPIN' ON THE "ONE"

Remember the special "one" beat we discussed in chapter 4? Now we're going to put that puppy to work.

You'll need two copies of the same song, one on each deck. (If you use two different songs, make sure they're the same bpm.)

EXERCISE 23: DROPPIN' ON THE "ONE"

1. Put the mixer's crossfader in the center and both volume faders up at full volume.

2. Set the pitch controls to "0" (in the middle) on both decks.

3. Cue up both songs to the first beat.

4. If using records, mark the start point with a sticker on the label at twelve o'clock. If using CDJs, take a visual note of the line position on the jog wheel display. If using a controller with software, look at the sound wave to find your start point.

5. Hold the record (or jog wheel) on the right deck (Song B) with your right hand to keep the first beat in place and press PLAY, but don't let go of the song. If using a controller with software, look at the sound wave to find your start point.

6. Start playing the song on the left deck (Song A) by pushing the START button with your left hand.

7. Let Song A play for seven bars: 1, 2, 3, 4 | 2, 2, 3, 4 | 3, 2, 3, 4 | 4, 2, 3, 4 | 5, 2, 3, 4 | 6, 2, 3, 4 | 7, 2, 3, 4 .

8. Perform four baby scratches using the first beat of Song B on the eighth bar with your right hand: 8, 2, 3, 4 (baby, baby, baby, baby).

9. Release Song B on the "one" of Song A's next bar, which is the beginning of the next eight-bar phrase: 1, 2, 3, 4 …

10. Let Song B play together with Song A for four bars: 1, 2, 3, 4 | 2, 2, 3, 4 | 3, 2, 3, 4 | 4, 2, 3, 4.

11. On the fifth bar, rewind Song B back to the start point as fast as you can and hold your hand in the nine o'clock position on the record (or jog wheel). Check the visual start point to ensure you are holding it in the right place.

12. While you're rewinding Song B, Song A continues to play through most of the eight-bar phrase: 5, 2, 3, 4 | 6, 2, 3, 4 | 7, 2, 3, 4 .

13. Repeat steps eight through twelve throughout the rest of Song A.

14. Do the entire exercise again, but this time switch sides and play Song B while dropping in Song A.

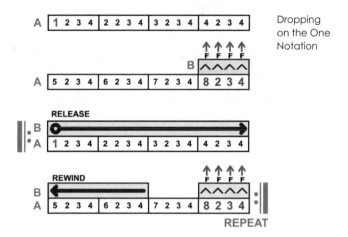

Dropping on the One Notation

TIP: The smaller the babies, the more precise you'll be able to drop it on beat. Watch the visual marker for the most exact drop!

TIP: You can also try all these beat dropping exercises by just pressing the start and rewind buttons on your controller or CDJs!

BABY-RELEASE-REWIND COMBO WITH CROSSFADER

Sometimes you don't want the dance floor to hear your baby scratches when you are about to drop in the next beat. You never want them to hear your rewinds (unless you're performing some snazzy trick!) Use the crossfader like an on/off switch to make silent babies and rewinds ninja style!

EXERCISE 24: BABY-RELEASE-REWIND COMBO WITH CROSSFADER (SILENT BABIES AND REWINDS)

1. Set both volume faders up at full volume.

2. Put on your headphones and set them to cue so you can hear the right deck.

3. Take one headphone off one ear so you can also hear the speakers.

4. Cue up Song B to the first beat on the right deck and hold at nine o'clock.

5. Set crossfader all the way to the left side ("off" position) and hold.

Crossfader with Left, Hold Record with Right   Crossfader with Left, Baby with Right

6. Perform four baby scratches "silently" in the headphones by moving the record (or jog wheel) forward and back four times. (This should only be heard in the headphones, *not* on the speakers!)

7. Push the crossfader to the middle ("on" position) and let go of Song B at the same time. (Don't let go of crossfader, just hold it in the middle.)

Crossfader in Middle, Release with Right   Crossfader on Left, Rewind with Right

8. Let Song B play for four beats: 1, 2, 3, 4.

9. Push crossfader back to the left side ("off" position) and hold.

10. Rewind the song back to its start point "silently" in headphones and hold at nine o'clock.

11. Repeat steps six through ten until you master this!

DROPPIN' ON THE "ONE" USING THE CROSSFADER AND HEADPHONES

Let's put it all together!

EXERCISE 25: DROPPIN' ON THE "ONE" USING THE CROSS-FADER AND HEADPHONES (SILENT BABIES AND REWINDS)

1. Set both volume faders at full volume.

2. Set the pitch controls on both decks to "0" (in the middle).

3. Put on your headphones and set the headphone cue to hear both songs.

4. Take one headphone off one ear so you can also hear the speakers.

5. Cue up both songs to the first beat.

6. If using records, mark the start point with a sticker on the label at twelve o'clock. If using CDJs, take a visual note of the line position on the jog wheel display. If using a controller with software, look at the sound wave to find your start point.

7. Hold the record (or jog wheel) on the right deck (Song B) with your right hand to keep the first beat in place.

8. Push the crossfader all the way to the left side with your left hand ("off" position).

9. Start playing the song on the left deck (Song A) by pushing the START button with your left hand.

10. Let Song A play for seven bars: 1, 2, 3, 4 | 2, 2, 3, 4 | 3, 2, 3, 4 | 4, 2, 3, 4 | 5, 2, 3, 4 | 6, 2, 3, 4 | 7, 2, 3, 4.

11. Using the first beat of Song B, perform four baby scratches "silently" on the eighth bar of Song A : 8, 2, 3, 4 (baby, baby, baby, baby). This should only be heard in the headphones, not in the speakers!

12. Push the crossfader to the middle with left hand ("on" position) and simultaneously release Song B on the "one" of Song A's next bar, which is the beginning of the next eight-bar phrase: 1, 2, 3, 4.

13. Let Song B play together with Song A for four bars: 1, 2, 3, 4 | 2, 2, 3, 4 | 3, 2, 3, 4 | 4, 2, 3, 4.

14. On the fifth bar, push the crossfader back to the left side.

15. "Silently" rewind Song B back to the start point as fast as you can. Listen to it rewinding in your headphones and hold your hand in the nine o'clock position on the record (or jog wheel). This song should *not* be heard rewinding in the speakers!

16. Check the visual start point to ensure you are holding it in the right place.

17. While you're rewinding Song B, Song A continues to play through most of the eight-bar phrase: 5, 2, 3, 4 | 6, 2, 3, 4 | 7, 2, 3, 4.

18. Repeat steps eleven through eighteen throughout the rest of Song A.

19. Repeat the entire exercise, but this time switch sides and play Song B while dropping in Song A.

TIP: Slow rewinds make you miss your cue! Rewind as fast as you can until you don't hear anything and then fast-forward until you first hear sound and you're there!

6 MATCHING THE BEATS

Woo-hoo! It's time to beatmatch!

BEATMATCHING

Before you blend two songs together, you have to match their tempos by lining up their beats audibly.

Unmatched Beats   Matched Beats

I'm going to show you how to manually manipulate the song's speeds in various ways while listening in order to match their tempos. This will help you develop the right touch so that you can get your beats matched as quickly as possible.

DJ software programs, such as Serato Scratch Live, give you the ability to see the sound waves and align them side by side, which helps to match the beats visually. It's a great feature; however, it isn't totally reliable, so you have to be able to beatmatch with your ears first.

To get the most out of these lessons, if you're using software to provide the audio for your hardware (i.e., Serato Scratch Live with turntables or CDJs), cover your computer screen so that you can't see the sound waves. This forces you to only use your ears and will ultimately make you a better DJ!

If you're completely software-based, simply use the deck controls in the software as you would a piece of hardware, but cover any parts of the screen that might help you to beatmatch visually (i.e., sound waves).

You'll need two of the same song, one on each deck. (If using two different songs, make sure they're the same bpm.)

EXERCISE 26: MANUAL SPEED-UP METHOD

1. Play a song on the right deck and listen to its tempo.

2. If using a turntable, put your finger on the record label, press down, and gradually rotate it clockwise to speed up the record's rotation. Press down too hard and you'll stop the platter underneath. Don't press hard enough and you won't change the speed. Practice getting the right touch.

3. If using a CDJ or controller, turn the jog wheel clockwise in a steady motion to speed up the song's rotation.

4. Notice when you stop speeding it up, the song returns to its normal speed.

5. Keep your speed adjustment as steady as possible while experimenting with different amounts of pressure and/or rotation rates.

6. Notice the differences in how gradually or quickly you can speed the song up. If you do it too fast, you'll skip a beat. It's all about control.

7. Now try to maintain a certain speed and see how long you can keep it spinning at that rate.

8. Repeat the entire exercise with your left hand on the left deck.

Speed Up Record with Label   Speed Up CD with Jog Wheel

EXERCISE 27: MANUAL SLOW-DOWN METHOD

1. Play a song on the right deck and listen to its tempo.

2. If using a turntable, rest your finger against the side of the platter. Let it rub against the platter and press down so that it slows the record down. Press too hard and you'll stop the platter. Don't press hard enough and you won't change the speed. Practice getting the right touch.

3. If using a CDJ or controller, turn the jog wheel counter-clockwise in a steady motion to slow down the song.

4. Notice when you stop slowing it down, the song returns to its normal speed.

5. Keep your speed adjustment as steady as possible while experimenting with different amounts of pressure or jog wheel rotation rates.

6. Notice the differences in how quickly or gradually you can slow the song down.

7. Now try to maintain a certain speed and see how long you can keep it spinning at that rate.

8. Repeat the entire exercise with your left hand on the left deck.

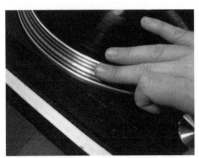

Slow Down Record with Platter   Slow Down CD with Jog Wheel

EXERCISE 28: USING MANUAL ADJUSTMENTS

1. Set both volume faders up at full volume and crossfader in the middle.

2. Set the pitch controls on both decks to "0" (in the middle).

3. Cue up both songs to the first beat.

4. Hold the record (or jog wheel) on the right deck (Song B) with your right hand to keep the first beat in place.

5. Start playing the song on the left deck (Song A).

6. Drop Song B on the "one" beat of Song A's next eight-bar phrase. Use baby scratches and try to drop it exactly on beat. (See exercise 23: Droppin' on the "One")

7. Listen to both beats playing at the same time. Do both beats sound in sync with each other? If not, you have to make an adjustment and proceed to step eight. However, if the beats sound synced, do a happy dance, and skip to step twelve!

8. Listen and try to figure out if Song B is playing ahead or lagging behind Song A. If you can't tell, just guess! You have a 50-50 chance of getting it right!

9. If Song B sounds like it's lagging behind Song A, use the manual speed-up method to speed it up. If you speed it up too much, or it sounds like its getting worse, no worries—just slow it down using the manual slow-down method.

10. If Song B sounds like it's playing ahead of Song A, use the manual slow-down method to slow it down. If you slow it down too much, no worries—just speed it up using the manual speed-up method.

11. Continue adjusting until the beats are exactly in sync. See how long you can keep them on with each other.

12. If you dropped Song B exactly on beat from the start, good for you!! Now mess it up so it's off beat with Song A and try getting it back on beat.

13. Repeat the entire exercise, but this time switch sides and play Song B while dropping in Song A.

WHAT TO LISTEN FOR

Listen for drum sounds that appear in both songs and try to match 'em up with each other. For example, when I beatmatch house music, I listen for the kick drums on all four beats (1, 2, 3, 4), but in hip-hop I match up the snare drums on beats two and four (—, 2, —, 4). It all depends on the music, so the more you know your tunes the easier it is to know what sounds to listen for in each song.

HOW TO TELL IF THE SONG IS TOO FAST OR TOO SLOW

When you first start out, your ears aren't tuned yet, so it's mostly trial and error. The good news is there are only two choices: speed it up or slow it down.

Listen closely and make an adjustment based on what you think you hear. If you have no idea, just guess! Don't worry about making the wrong choice because it will always tell you what the right choice is. The worst thing you can do is nothing because you won't give yourself any clues. Make a move, any move!

For example, let's say the record is actually too slow but you can't tell by listening, so you make an adjustment to give yourself a clue. If you choose to slow it down, it will sound worse, like the beats are getting further apart, and now you'll know for sure that you need to speed it up. However, if you choose to speed it up, it will sound better, like the beats are getting closer together, and you'll know for sure you're on the right track.

It takes time and practice to tune your ears, but once you've got it, you've got it!

TIP: Always focus on adjusting only one song at a time to ensure that the other song stays constant. If you mess with both songs at the same time, it can get confusing.

EXERCISE 29: CONTINUOUS MANUAL SPEEDUP

1. Set both volume faders up at full volume and crossfader in the middle.

2. Set the pitch control on the left deck to "0" (in the middle).

3. Set the pitch control on the right deck to "-4"

Pitch -4

4. Cue up both songs to the first beat.

5. Hold the record (or jog wheel) on the right deck (Song B) with your right hand to keep the first beat in place.

6. Start playing the song on the left deck (Song A).

7. Drop Song B on the "one" beat of Song A's next eight-bar phrase. Use your baby scratches and try to drop it exactly on beat.

8. Listen to both beats playing at the same time. Notice Song B is slowing down.

9. Manually speed up Song B by using the manual speed-up method.

10. Try to get Song B up to the speed of Song A and then keep it there as long as you can.

11. If you speed up Song B too much then, let go for a bit until it matches up with Song A and resume speeding up manually to keep it in time with Song A.

12. If you totally mess up and the beats are all over the place (aka "train wreck"), then cue up Song B back to the first beat and start over again, dropping Song B on the "one" of Song A's next eight-bar phrase.

13. Try to manually keep Song B up to speed with Song A throughout the entire song.

14. Repeat the entire exercise, but this time switch sides and play Song B (set pitch control of right deck at "0") while dropping in Song A (set pitch control on left deck at "-4").

EXERCISE 30: CONTINUOUS MANUAL SLOWDOWN

1. Set both volume faders up at full volume and crossfader in the middle.

2. Set the pitch control on the left deck to "0" (in the middle).

3. Set the pitch control on the right deck to "+4."

Pitch +4

4. Cue up both songs to the first beat.

5. Hold the record (or jog wheel) on the right deck (Song B) with your right hand to keep the first beat in place.

6. Start playing the song on the left deck (Song A).

7. Drop Song B on the "one" beat of Song A's next eight-bar phrase. Use your baby scratches and try to drop it exactly on beat.

8. Listen to both beats playing at the same time. Notice Song B is speeding up.

9. Manually slow down Song B by using the manual slow-down method.

10. Try to slow Song B down to the speed of Song A and then keep it there as long as you can.

11. If you slow down Song B too much, then let go for a bit until it matches up with Song A, and resume slowing down manually to keep it in time with Song A.

12. If you totally mess up and the beats are all over the place (aka "train wreck"), then cue up Song B back to the first beat and start over again, dropping Song B on the "one" of Song A's next eight-bar phrase.

13. Try to manually keep Song B slowed down with Song A throughout the entire song.

14. Repeat the entire exercise, but this time switch sides and play Song B (set pitch control of right deck at "0") while dropping in Song A (set pitch control on left deck at "+4").

EXERCISE 31: FULL PITCH ADJUSTMENTS
You will need a 3" x 6" piece of paper, folded in half lengthwise.

1. Set both volume faders up at full volume and crossfader in the middle.

2. Set the pitch control on the right deck to "0" (in the middle).

3. Close your eyes, blindly move the pitch control on the left deck to an unknown setting, and cover the pitch control so you can't see it. (No peeking!)

Paper Covering Pitch Control

4. Cue up both songs to the first beat.

5. Hold the record (or jog wheel) on the right deck (Song B) with your right hand to keep the first beat in place.

6. Start playing the song on the left deck (Song A).

7. Listen to Song A. Does it sound faster or slower than its normal speed?

8. Drop Song B on the "one" beat of Song A's next eight-bar phrase. Use your baby scratches and try to drop it exactly on beat.

9. Listen carefully to both beats playing at the same time. Is Song B speeding up or slowing down?

10. Make a decision and act on it by manually speeding up Song B or slowing it down. If you can't decide, just guess, and do it fast before the beats become a train wreck. If they train-wreck, cue up Song B back to the

first beat and start over again. (Get used to this because you'll be doing it often!)

11. Okay, so you made a move, but was it the right one? Are the beats getting closer together or further apart? If the beats sound like they're getting closer, stay with it. If they sound further apart, do the opposite.

12. Can you keep Song B on with your manual adjustments? If so, it means the two songs are pretty close in tempo. Just move the pitch control of Song B up (+) or down (-) depending on what manual adjustments you're making. For example, if you're speeding the song up manually and can keep it on, then bump the pitch up one or two notches (+) and listen to see if it stays on.

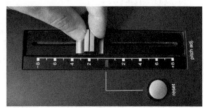
Moving Pitch Control

13. Or does it sound like they're getting closer but still too far off to keep it on manually? This means the two songs are further apart from each other, so you have to adjust the pitch so they're closer. For example, if you're slowing the song down manually but you can't keep it on, then move down (-) the pitch control of Song B about three or four notches, and then see if it's easier to keep it on manually. If it is, then keep adjusting the pitch until you no longer have to do it manually and listen to see if it stays on.

14. In either case, the beats might get totally off and train-wreck while you're adjusting. This doesn't necessarily mean you're off track with your course of action. It may just mean you weren't able to adjust it fast enough. If this happens, just cue up Song B back to the first beat, drop it in again, and listen to see how close it is to Song A.

15. If the beats sound further apart, reassess the situation and make a different adjustment. If it gets off, cue it up and drop it in again. It's always easier to start from square one to make a clear assessment and go from there.

16. If the beats sound closer, it means you're on the right track. Keep manually adjusting and then following up with a pitch-control adjustment until you get it on beat. If it gets off, cue it up and drop it in again.

17. Listen. Assess. Make an adjustment. Listen. Assess. Make an adjustment. Keep making manual adjustments and then solidifying them by moving the pitch closer to the speed you think it should be. This may take some time and Song A may even run out. If that happens, just rewind Song

A to the beginning, drop Song B on the "one," and keep going until you get the beats matched with each other.

18. Once the songs sound in sync and you think they're beatmatched, just listen to see if they stay on. If they drift, make a manual adjustment and listen again. If they drift again, adjust the pitch control ever so slightly in the correct direction. Sometimes a tiny tap one way or the other is all you need!

19. If it's really close, be careful of over-adjusting with the pitch. You may just need to make a final manual tweak to get it on. However, if you move the pitch when all you needed was a tiny manual adjustment with your hand, then you might be moving it further way from where it should be.

20. Once you get your beats matched and they don't drift apart, let them play together for a while and do a happy dance. *You did it!* Lift up the paper from the left pitch control and compare to the right one to see how close you got!

21. Repeat the entire exercise again and again and again and again. ...

TIP: Your manual adjustments are mainly to figure out what course of action you should take (speed up or slow down), but you have to solidify your actions by moving the pitch control one way or the other; otherwise, the song will go back to its original playing speed once you stop manually adjusting it.

EXERCISE 32: DIFFERENT SONGS
Complete the four previous beatmatching exercises using two *different* songs with the same bpm.

EXERCISE 33: DIFFERENT SONGS, DIFFERENT BPM
Complete Exercise 31: Full Pitch Adjustments using two *different* songs with *different* bpm. Make sure the bpm are within a workable range. (See the bpm section in chapter 4). If you can pull this off, you're in!

7 MIXING IT UP

Congrats! Now that you can officially beatmatch, it's time to mix the songs together and *spin now*!

LEVEL ADJUSTMENTS

Before you mix a new song in, adjust its volume so it's the same level as the song playing out on the dance floor.

To do this, switch back and forth between the songs in your headphones to compare volumes, and then adjust the new song using the gain.

Right Volume Meter Too Low

You should also compare the LED lights (volume meters) for each channel on the mixer. If the new song's volume is lower than the other song, the lights display lower. If it's louder, the lights display higher. Adjust it so they both hit the same spot.

Right Volume Meter Too High

If either channel shows red bars, it means the music is too loud and the sound will distort. Ideally they should stay out of the red entirely.

If both channels are in the red, it means the gains are cranked up to high. Turn them down so they're out of the red, and then turn mixer's master volume up louder to balance it out. This ensures the best possible sound quality.

Even Volume Meters

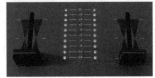

Both Volume Meters in Red

SIMPLE BLEND

A simple blend is fading one song into another and then fading the other song out.

EXERCISE 34: SIMPLE BLEND

1. Set the crossfader in the middle, the left volume fader up at full volume, and the right volume fader all the way down.

2. Start playing Song A on the left deck.

3. Cue Song B on the right deck using the headphones.

4. Beatmatch Song B with Song A.

5. Cue Song B back to the first beat.

6. Drop Song B on the "one" of a phrase in Song A.

7. Start gradually fading in Song B by moving the right channel volume fader up with your left hand. The smoother the better, no jerky movements.

Fading In

8. If Song B starts to drift off beat, use your right hand to make manual adjustments and keep it on beat with Song A.

9. Fade Song B all the way up. Both songs should be playing at full volume in the speakers.

Full Volume

10. If Song B still seems quieter than Song A, raise the gain level for the right channel until the levels match up. If Song B seems too loud, lower the gain level for the right channel.

11. Listen to your mix for at least eight bars while keeping the records on beat with each other.

12. Do a happy dance.

13. Start to gradually fade out Song A by smoothly moving the left volume fader down with your left hand until it's completely out of the mix.

14. Do another dance and repeat the exercise with different songs.

TIP: Always fade the new song all the way in before fading out the previous one. If you begin to fade out the previous song too early, there'll be a dip in the overall volume and your mix wont sound even.

BASIC EQ MIX

This basic mix adjusts the bass frequencies to create a smoother mix. The bass is the strongest frequency. When mixing two songs with full bass at the same time, the mix gets louder and may distort when they are both at full volume, and then gets quieter when one song plays by itself. To avoid these unwanted peaks and valleys, switch the bass frequencies during your mix to keep it on an even plane. This technique can also be applied to any of the other frequencies, so feel free to experiment once you get the hang of it!

EXERCISE 35: BASIC EQ MIX

1. Set the crossfader in the middle, the left volume fader up at full volume and the right volume fader all the way down.
2. Set all EQs straight up at twelve o'clock.
3. Start playing Song A on the left deck.
4. Cue Song B on the right deck using the headphones.
5. Beatmatch Song B with Song A.
6. Cue Song B back to the first beat.
7. Turn the bass knob on the right channel all the way down to zero, taking all the bass out of Song B.
8. Drop Song B on the "one" of a phrase in Song A.
9. Start gradually fading in Song B by moving the right channel volume fader up with your left hand. The smoother the better, no jerky movements.
10. If Song B starts to drift off beat, use your right hand to make manual adjustments and keep it on beat with Song A.
11. Fade Song B all the way up. Both songs should be playing at full volume in the speakers.
12. Adjust the gain for Song B if necessary, but keep in mind that it has no bass and once the bass is added it will seem much louder.
13. Start to gradually fade in the bass frequency of Song B on the right channel by turning the knob clockwise with your right hand.

14. Once you get the bass knob to about nine o'clock, start turning down the bass knob on the left channel counter-clockwise with your left hand.

15. Continue switching them until the right bass knob is at twelve o'clock and the left bass knob is at nine o'clock. This process should be slow and smooth.

16. Continue turning the left bass knob all the way to zero.

Fading Bass Nine O'clock

17. Listen to your mix for at least eight bars more while keeping the records on beat with each other.

18. Do a happy dance.

Fading Both Bass Knobs

19. Start to gradually fade out Song A by smoothly moving the left volume fader down with your left hand until it's completely out of the mix.

20. Do another dance and repeat the exercise with different songs.

DROP MIX USING EQ

A drop mix is a more advanced mix that is used to get in and out faster. This mix will span over a quick eight bars and incorporates a faster version of an EQ mix to spice things up. If it feels too fast for you try, double the allotted bars to sixteen until you get the hang of it. If you're feeling really brave, try four bars!

You'll use the crossfader to cut Song B in at half volume. This cutting technique without the baby scratch is more advanced, so feel free to practice it a few times before you start.

EXERCISE 36: CUTTING

1. Cue up Song B on the right deck.

2. Set crossfader all the way to the left side.

3. Hold crossfader with left hand and Song B with right hand.

4. Push the crossfader to the middle and let go of Song B at the same time.

Crossfader Left/Hold Song Right   Crossfader Middle/Release Song Right

EXERCISE 37: DROP MIX USING EQ

1. Set the crossfader all the way to the left side, the left volume fader up at full volume, and the right volume fader all the way down.

2. All EQs should be pointing straight up at twelve o'clock.

3. Start playing Song A on the left deck.

4. Cue Song B on the right deck using the headphones.

5. Beatmatch Song B with Song A.

6. Cue Song B back to the first beat.

7. Set the right volume fader half way up.

8. Push the crossfader to the middle with left hand and let go of Song B at the same time with right hand, dropping it on the "one" of an eight-bar phrase in Song A. (Or you can do four "silent baby scratches" and then drop it in with the crossfader.)

Cutting in half volume

9. Start quickly but smoothly fading in Song B by moving the right channel volume fader up with your right hand. You have the full eight bars to get this all the way up.

10. While fading up Song B, start to turn the left channel's bass frequency down for Song A with your left hand (the bass should be close to zero by the time the mix is finished).

Fade Volume Up and Bass Down at the Same Time

11. If Song B starts to drift off beat, use your right hand to make manual adjustments and keep it on beat with Song A.

Cut Volume

12. After the full eight bars finish, cut Song A's volume fader all the way down to zero. Ideally this cut should happen on the "one" of the next phrase (i.e., beat one of the ninth bar)

13. Song B should remain playing full volume on the dance floor.

14. Wipe the sweat off your brow, do a happy dance, and repeat the exercise with different songs.

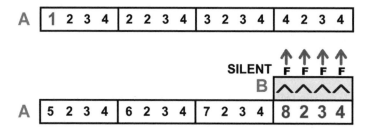

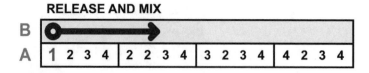

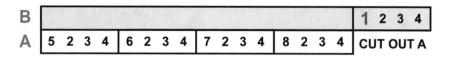

Drop Mix Notation

8 WHAT'S NEXT?

PRACTICE! PRACTICE! PRACTICE!

You made it through the book! Hooray! Now go forth and practice your butt off like there's no tomorrow because that's the only way to become great. You want every move you make to become second nature, so you don't even have to think about it. The best DJs spend countless hours practicing their skills so that when they are in a live setting, their talent just flows freely and they are able to handle anything that is thrown at them.

RECORD YOURSELF

Record yourself practicing and then listen to it. It's a lot easier to hear what you're doing when you aren't actually doing it. Just hit record and play for an hour, totally unplanned. You'll hear what worked and what didn't so you'll know what to do next time.

You can also create planned DJ mixes and record them. Spend time putting together a series of mixes just like a puzzle so you know exactly when to bring them in and out. Once you have the whole thing planned, record it. This forces you to mix each mix over and over until you get it perfect. Once you are done, you've upped your skill level and you end up with a killer recorded mix to promote your awesome skills with!

PLAY FOR YOUR HOMIES

If you are nervous about performing in front of a crowd, don't stress. Just start practicing in front of other people early on to help conquer your fear. Start small, just one close friend who loves you and has your back. Then invite a group of friends over and DJ for them or even throw a house party and provide the music. This will help you get used to having people in the room while you're performing so that when you score that first gig, you're more than ready for it.

DJing your own house party is also a great way to practice because it gives you the feel of being in an active room with loud music, yet allows you to make mistakes and learn from them in a safe environment.

BUILD YOUR FAN BASE!

You can be the greatest thing since sliced bread, but if nobody knows you exist, you won't get very far!

WHAT'S YO NAME?

If you haven't done this already, you need to pick a DJ name. It can be your own name or something totally different that you make up for yourself. Think of your DJ name as your alter ego. It should be a memorable name that you love, which represents you in some way.

Once you find a name that you like, do your research to make sure no one else has it! If another well-known DJ/producer already has the name, they will definitely appear on an Internet search, in which case, you should go back to the drawing board. For example, when I chose my name, I made sure that I was the first and only one to use it and I chose to spell it *Shortee* with two *ee*'s just in case someone else got the bright idea in the future!

Once you pick your original name, buy the URL (i.e., www.djshortee.com) and reserve your name space on every social media site you can think of to start building your profiles (Facebook, Twitter, MySpace, YouTube, SoundCloud, and so on). Even if you don't immediately create your profiles or have the means to build a website, you at least want to own your name in all these areas so no one else can use it. URLs are super cheap and the profiles are free, so what are you waiting for?

CREATING AWARENESS

Build all your online profiles, create a simple website, and post your DJ mixes for free download so others can hear them. Once you gain a few fans, they will start sharing your mixes with their friends. All you have to do is interact with them and treat them like gold and they will be fans for life.

Go to the venues that you would like to play at and pass out your mix CDs to anyone that will take one. Of course, you'll want to give one to the club owner or promoters, but also pass them out to the audience to start building your fan base. Go to local shops that cater to your music scene and drop off a stack of your CDs for them to give away for free.

If you really want to go the extra mile, learn how to produce remixes and original tracks and post them online for free download. If you are able to get them signed to a label that caters to your music, it'll propel your name quickly to a much wider audience worldwide.

PLAYING OUT!

Your best promotion is your live show so make it good every single time! Treat each gig like it's your last and never forget how lucky you are to be able to have this amazing opportunity!

BE PREPARED!

If you play on turntables, bring your own slipmats and needles. You never know what you are going to end up with, so it's best to have your own. If you are a nightclub DJ, bring an extra light with you so you can see if it's super dark. If you play on DJ software, bring an extra vinyl record or CD to use when switching to your computer, if needed. Oh, and this should go without saying, but always bring your own headphones. You never want to have to borrow a dripping-wet pair from the sweaty DJ that just played before you, ew!

Before you play your first song, check *everything*. Check every button, knob, plug, and fader. Make sure it is all working correctly and set how you like it. If you are going on after another DJ, they may have maxed out the volumes or changed all the settings, so if you go on without fixing it, it may sound distorted or things may not work right.

MISTAKES

Mistakes are going to happen, but they will ultimately make you a better DJ, and the longer you're in the game, the fewer there will be. If you make a mistake, don't worry—just keep going and finish strong. Don't advertise it to the audience because they probably didn't even notice it anyway. Sometimes mistakes can be a good, and you create something live that was completely unexpected and totally awesome! Embrace the mistakes. It just shows the audience that you're a human being performing live instead of a programmed computer and they'll ultimately respect you for it.

DON'T BE AN ASS!

Always be professional and courteous with the promoters and club owners. No one wants to book someone that's a pain in the butt to deal with. Most of all, treat your fans with respect, mingle with the crowd and thank them for coming out to see you play! Without them, you would be playing to an empty room! Nuff said.

HAVE FUN!

Ultimately, DJing is all about the music and having fun. If it's not fun, then what's the point? Just be yourself, play music you love, and enjoy the experience. If you're having fun, the crowd will feel your energy and ride that wave with you. You're literally controlling the crowd, taking them on a musical journey, and that's incredibly powerful! Love what you do and rock those decks!

ABOUT THE DVD-ROM

The accompanying DVD-ROM is to be used together with certain featured exercises throughout *Spin Now!* When the DVD logo is located next to an exercise in the text, watch the indicated clip for a more detailed version of the lesson.

The videos are organized into two folders, entitled "CDJs" and "Turntables," so those who are primarily interested in learning to DJ using CDs can skip past all of the turntable exercises, and vice versa.

TRACK LIST FOR CDJS AND TURNTABLES FOLDERS

1. Intro
2. Exercise 20: Baby Scratch
3. Exercise 21: Release Scratch
4. Exercise 22: Baby Release Combo
5. Exercise 23: Droppin' on the "One"
6. Exercise 24: Baby Release with Crossfader
7. Exercise 25: Droppin' on the "One" with Crossfader and Headphones
8. Exercise 26: Manual Speed Up Method
9. Exercise 27: Manual Slow Down Method
10. Exercise 28: Using Manual Adjustments
11. Exercise 29: Continuous Manual Speed Up Method
12. Exercise 29: Continuous Manual Slow Down Method
13. Exercise 31: Full Pitch Adjustments
14. Exercise 34: Simple Blend
15. Exercise 35: Basic EQ Mix
16. Exercise 36: Cutting
17. Exercise 37: Drop Mix Using EQ

Note: This DVD-ROM will not play in a standard DVD player. To view the video tutorials on your computer, tablet, or smartphone, simply import them from the DVD-ROM directly into iTunes, Windows Media Player, QuickTime Player, or any other full-featured media playback application.

VINYL RECORDS USED

» Turntable Exercises 20–31: *Shortee & Step 1,* "Bikini Wax"

» Turntable Exercises 34–37: *Shortee,* "Shortee's DJ Workshop"

DIGITAL MUSIC USED

» CDJ Exercises 20–31: *Urban Assault,* "Dope" (Drumstep Mix)

» CDJ Exercises 34–35: *Faust & Shortee,* "Hustlers"

» CDJ Exercises 34–35: *Faust & Shortee,* "C'mon"

» CDJ Exercises 36–37: *Urban Assault,* "Dope" (Jeep Beats Mix)

DVD CREDITS

» Filmed and edited by Brian Pucher and Amir Tarazkar

» Written and directed by DJ Shortee

» All records and music used in the lessons can be purchased at the Heavy Artillery Recordings online store (www.heavyartilleryrecordings.com).